Copyright © 2017 by Herald Entertainment, Inc., McKinney, TX
All Rights Reserved
Illustrations by Herald Entertainment, Inc.
Visit our Brother Francis series website at: www.brotherfrancisonline.com
Printed in China
First Printing: August 2017
ISBN: 978-1-939182-74-6

THE STATIONS OF THE CROSS

Accompanying Jesus on His Way to Calvary

Hi! I was just enjoying the beautiful stars and thanking God for the gift of creation! You know, sometimes we take things for granted until we stop to think about them. It's like our salvation. We are thankful for it, but until we stop and think about what it cost Jesus to provide it for us, we may not be as thankful as we should be. One way to appreciate what Christ has done for us is by The Stations of the Cross.

  Join me as we accompany Jesus, our Savior, on His way to the cross where He gave His life for you and me.

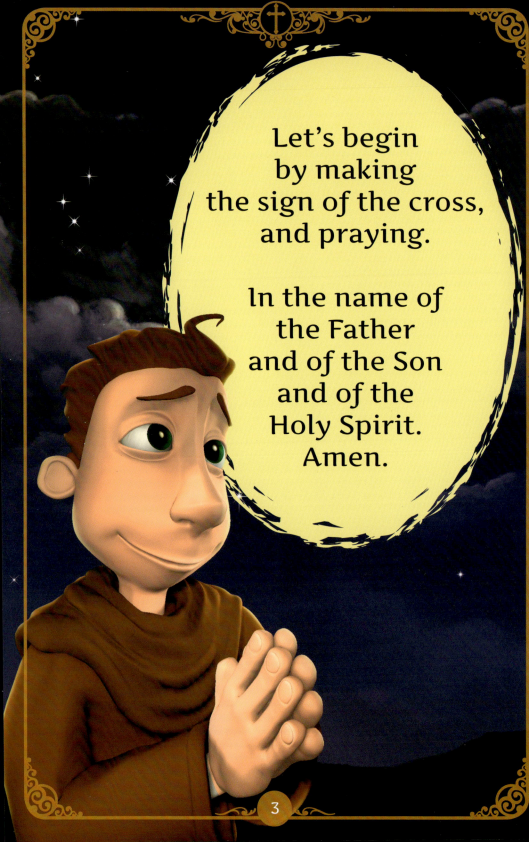

Dear God, You loved the world so much that You sent Your only Son, Jesus, so that we who believe in Him may have eternal life.

Bless us with the gift of grace, as we think about His journey toward the sacrifice that would bring forgiveness of sins through His suffering and death.

As we walk this path with Jesus, please bring us close to Him. We ask this through Jesus Christ, our Lord.

Amen.

MEDITATION ON STATION 1

Jesus, our Lord, stands before Pilate having been brought there by the religious leaders. Just days before, He had been praised by the people of the city, and now He stands before the governor, accused of many things. Pilate questions Him, and Jesus remains silent. The crowds call out for His death, and still our Lord is silent. Pilate, wanting to please the crowd, condemns our Lord to death.

RESPONSE :

Jesus, You were silent when You were condemned to the cross. You were silent because You were going to die for my salvation. Help me never forget Your sacrifice. Help me be as patient and loving with those around me. Jesus, our Lord…

ALL :
Have mercy on us.

PRAY: 1 Our Father, 1 Hail Mary, 1 Glory Be

MEDITATION ON STATION 2

Having been whipped, beaten, and made fun of, Jesus is humiliated even further by being made to carry the cross on which He is to die. Weak and in pain from all that has been inflicted upon Him, our Lord takes up His cross. It is very heavy, but not as heavy as the weight of our sins. Then He is led to the Place of the Skull, which in Hebrew is called Golgotha, to be put to death.

RESPONSE :

Loving Jesus, You carried my sins with You to the cross. You knew every sin I would ever commit and still You carried that cross for me. Thank You for that love. Jesus, our Lord...

ALL :
Have mercy on us.

PRAY: 1 Our Father, 1 Hail Mary, 1 Glory Be

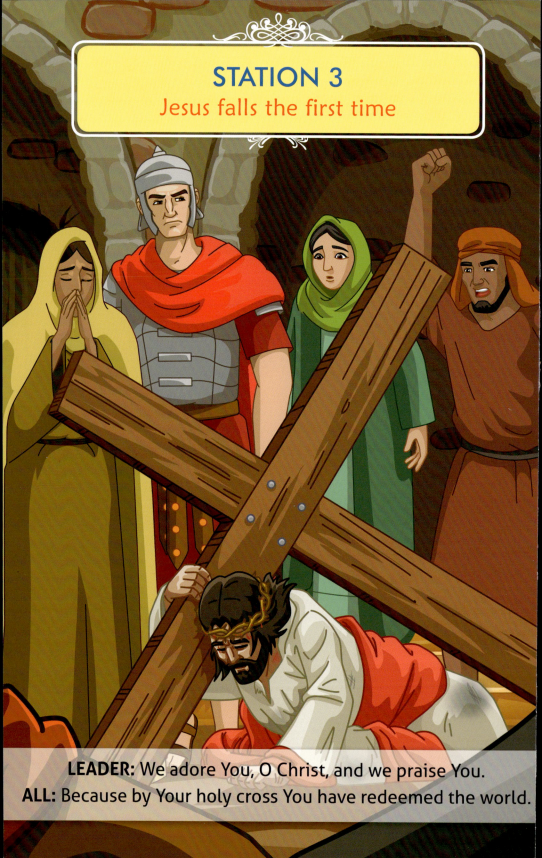

MEDITATION ON STATION 3

How difficult it must have been to carry the heavy weight of the cross upon shoulders that had been whipped and torn. As Jesus begins His journey to the place of execution, He makes His way through the city. Some people weep and others yell out insults. Suffering and exhausted, our Lord falls under the weight of the cross.

RESPONSE :

Lord, You bore the weight of my sins upon Your shoulders. If life weighs me down, please help me to remember that You understand. Jesus, our Lord...

ALL :
Have mercy on us.

PRAY: 1 Our Father, 1 Hail Mary, 1 Glory Be

STATION 4
Jesus meets His mother

LEADER: We adore You, O Christ, and we praise You.
ALL: Because by Your holy cross You have redeemed the world.

MEDITATION ON STATION 4

Rising once again, Jesus slowly makes His way through the narrow streets suffering in silence—suffering alone—until He looks up and sees a face among the multitude. It is a face streaming with tears. It is His mother. Brokenhearted, she approaches Him. She cannot stop what is happening, but Mary can share His sorrow.

RESPONSE :

Loving Jesus, when my own cross gets heavy, help me remember that I am not left alone. Help me to search for Your face, and that of Your mother's, even in the middle of my difficulties. Jesus, our Lord…

ALL :
Have mercy on us.

PRAY: 1 Our Father, 1 Hail Mary, 1 Glory Be

STATION 5
Simon of Cyrene helps Jesus to carry His cross

LEADER: We adore You, O Christ, and we praise You.
ALL: Because by Your holy cross You have redeemed the world.

MEDITATION ON STATION 5

Jesus falters in His steps. The Roman soldiers are impatient. They pull an onlooker from the crowd and force him to help Jesus carry the cross. The man's name is Simon and he is from Cyrene. Little does he know he is helping his own Savior and Lord.

RESPONSE :

Jesus, my help, be with me in my struggles and fears, and help me. Help me be a blessing to others in their time of need, as Simon was a help to You. Jesus, our Lord...

ALL :
Have mercy on us.

PRAY: 1 Our Father, 1 Hail Mary, 1 Glory Be

MEDITATION ON STATION 6

Every painful step takes Jesus closer to the edge of the city where He will suffer a cruel death. The agony is made more difficult by the insults He bears along the way. Then, from the crowd, a woman steps out. With great love, she wipes Jesus' face with a cloth. It is a moment of relief for our Lord. Miraculously, the image of His face remains on the fabric—a reminder of the love that drove Him to the cross for our salvation.

RESPONSE :

Loving and caring Jesus, Veronica did what others failed to do. When others oppose You, let me have the same courageous love to stand out from the crowd and serve You. Jesus, our Lord…

ALL :
Have mercy on us.

PRAY: 1 Our Father, 1 Hail Mary, 1 Glory Be

STATION 7
Jesus falls the second time

LEADER: We adore You, O Christ, and we praise You.
ALL: Because by Your holy cross You have redeemed the world.

MEDITATION ON STATION 7

The road to Golgotha is a difficult one and once again Jesus falls. The soldiers demand He rise again, and some of the people in the crowd are appalled by the way Jesus is treated. Others simply jeer at Him again. Slowly Jesus rises to His feet. His gaze is ahead to where He will fulfill what He has come to do—bring us salvation. He continues His way, one painful step after the other.

RESPONSE :

How it tears my heart to imagine what You suffered for me. Please give me strength in my own life so that in difficult times, I too may rise and continue my life one step at a time. Jesus, our Lord…

ALL :
Have mercy on us.

PRAY: 1 Our Father, 1 Hail Mary, 1 Glory Be

STATION 8
Jesus meets the women of Jerusalem

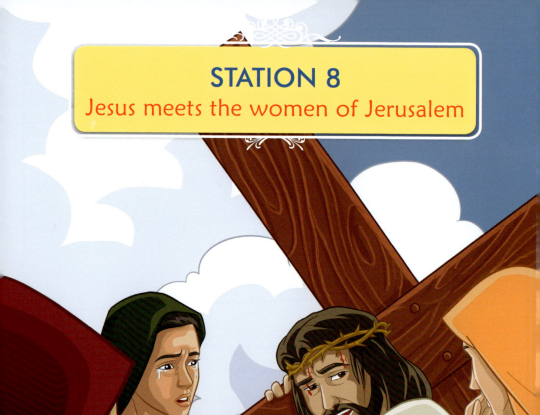

LEADER: We adore You, O Christ, and we praise You.
ALL: Because by Your holy cross You have redeemed the world.

MEDITATION ON STATION 8

As Jesus makes His way to the outskirts of the city, He is met by a group of women weeping at the sight of His suffering. Gazing upon them, Jesus tells them not to weep for Him but for those who do not recognize the work of God.

RESPONSE :

Dear Lord, how often I fail to see God at work in my life. Help me to take the time to be with You—to pray and to learn from You. Jesus, our Lord...

ALL :
Have mercy on us.

PRAY: 1 Our Father, 1 Hail Mary, 1 Glory Be

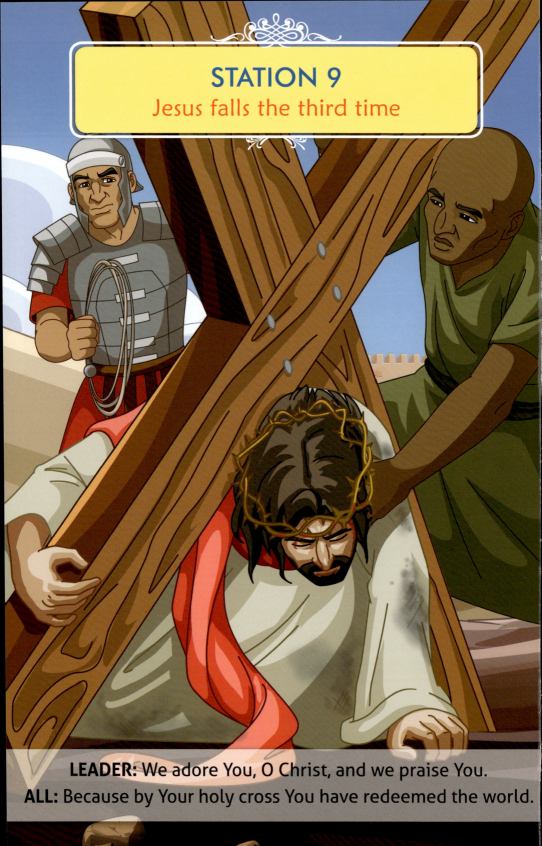

MEDITATION ON STATION 9

The place of His death is just ahead and the Lord struggles to reach it. He falls a third time. Once more He is forced to His feet and made to climb the hill where He, the Lamb of God, will take away the sins of the world.

RESPONSE :

Dear Jesus, sometimes I feel forgotten, yet how could I be, when You took so many steps of love for my benefit. Thank You. Jesus, our Lord...

ALL :
Have mercy on us.

PRAY: 1 Our Father, 1 Hail Mary, 1 Glory Be

STATION 10
Jesus' clothes are taken away

LEADER: We adore You, O Christ, and we praise You.
ALL: Because by Your holy cross You have redeemed the world.

MEDITATION ON STATION 10

Jesus has given everything. All that remains are the clothes He is wearing. In preparation for the crucifixion, they are taken off. Since His cloak has value, the soldiers throw dice for it, not realizing that the man that stands before them is of greater value than all creation. Jesus is silent, patient, and long-suffering.

RESPONSE :

Lord Jesus, You understand I am human. You understand my faults. Help me to value life more than material things. Jesus, our Lord...

ALL :
Have mercy on us.

PRAY: 1 Our Father, 1 Hail Mary, 1 Glory Be

STATION 11
Jesus is nailed to the cross

LEADER: We adore You, O Christ, and we praise You.
ALL: Because by Your holy cross You have redeemed the world.

MEDITATION ON STATION 11

Having reached the top of the hill, Jesus is made to lie on the cross. His arms are stretched out to both sides, His legs, to the foot of the cross. The soldiers take nails and crucify our Lord.

RESPONSE :

Merciful and loving Jesus, You love me like no one else has ever loved me before. Thank You for Your love and the sacrifice You made for me. Jesus, our Lord...

ALL :
Have mercy on us.

PRAY: 1 Our Father, 1 Hail Mary, 1 Glory Be

STATION 12
Jesus dies on the cross

LEADER: We adore You, O Christ, and we praise You.
ALL: Because by Your holy cross You have redeemed the world.

MEDITATION ON STATION 12

Having suffered on the cross for hours, the Lord cries out, "Father, into Your hands I commend My spirit!" Great darkness comes upon the land. In the temple the veil between the holy place and the holy of holies tears in two. Jesus has died.

RESPONSE :

Jesus, my Savior, help me never to forget what You have done for me. Jesus, our Lord...

ALL :
Have mercy on us.

PRAY: 1 Our Father, 1 Hail Mary, 1 Glory Be

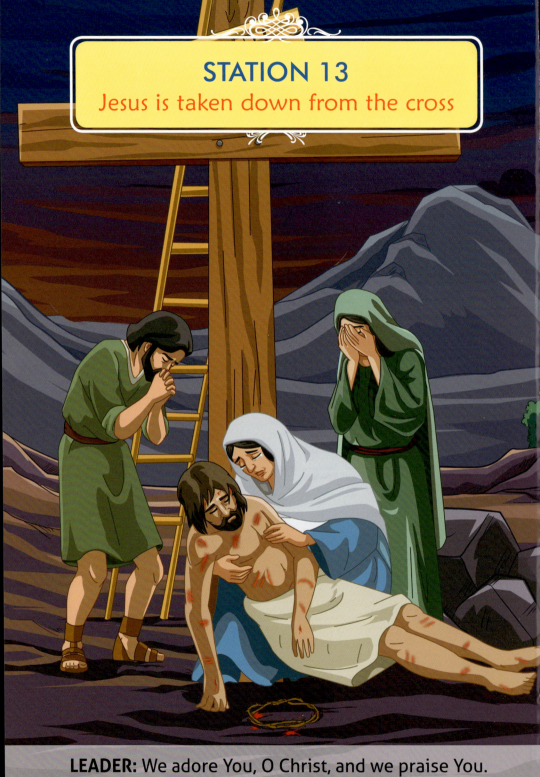

MEDITATION ON STATION 13

While some abandon our Lord in the time of His suffering, others do not. Jesus is taken down from the cross. He is placed on His grieving mother's lap. He is wept over and He is mourned. The Son of God came as a helpless child, and now, He lies upon the same lap. He has done what He came to do.

RESPONSE :
You gave all of Yourself for me, Lord. I give all there is of me to You. Jesus, our Lord...

ALL :
Have mercy on us.

PRAY: 1 Our Father, 1 Hail Mary, 1 Glory Be

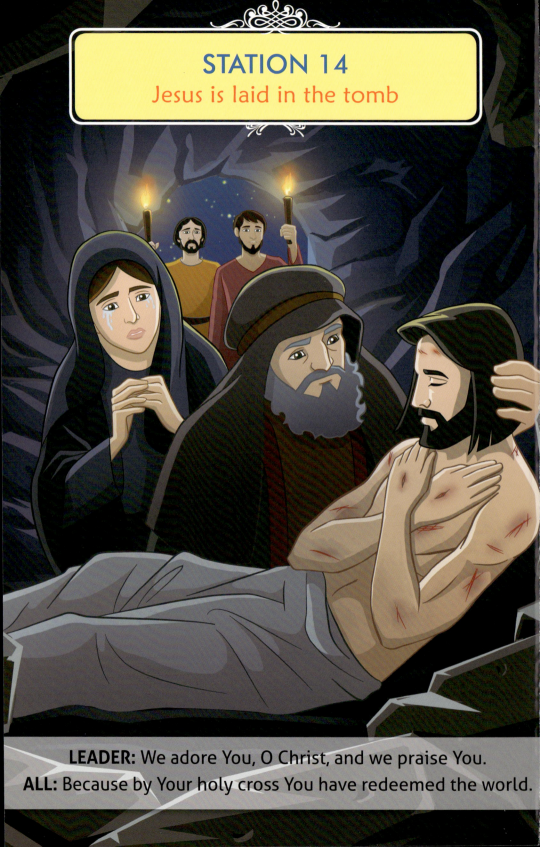

MEDITATION ON STATION 14

A wealthy man named Joseph of Arimathea, a follower of our Lord, has obtained permission from Pilate to take the body and prepare it for burial. With loving care, the body of Jesus is wrapped in linen and laid in a tomb.

RESPONSE :

When all is dark and seems hopeless, Lord, help me to remember that You died not only to be my Savior, but also King of my life. You died, that we may live. You are the resurrection and the life. Jesus, our Lord...

ALL :
Have mercy on us.

PRAY: 1 Our Father, 1 Hail Mary, 1 Glory Be

Jesus, You have united heaven and earth through the sacrifice of Your body and blood upon the cross. You have brought all those who believe in You to God, the Father. Help me to think often about what You did for my salvation and the salvation of the whole world.
Thank You, Jesus.
Amen.

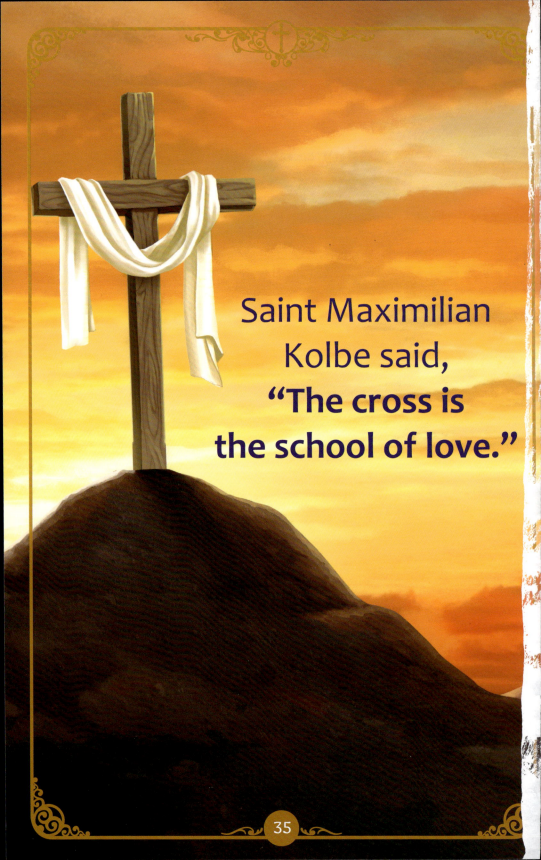